Left Out in the Rain

NEW POEMS 1947–1985

Gary Snyder

NORTH POINT PRESS
SAN FRANCISCO 1986

Some of the poems in this collection originally
appeared in somewhat different form in period-
ical publications, including *The Berkeley Bussei*,
CoEvolution Quarterly, *Combustion*, *Floating Bear*,
Hudson Review, *Janus*, *Kuksu*, *Occident*, *Scope*,
Sulfur, and *Yugen*; the author and publisher ex-
tend their thanks to these and any possibly for-
gotten fugitive publishers of these poems.

Cover photograph: Pamela Fong
Cover design: David Bullen

North Point Press
850 Talbot Avenue
Berkeley, California
94706

FOR DONALD ALLEN AND JAMES LAUGHLIN

Table of Contents

Left Out
in the Rain

Introduction

I

1947–1948

Elk Trails

Ancient, world-old Elk paths
Narrow, dusty Elk paths
Wide-trampled, muddy,
Aimless . . . wandering . . .
Everchanging Elk paths.

I have walked you, ancient trails,
Along the narrow rocky ridges
High above the mountains that
Make up your world:
Looking down on giant trees, silent
In the purple shadows of ravines—
Above the spire-like alpine fir
Above the high, steep-slanting meadows
Where sun-softened snowfields share the earth
With flowers.

I have followed narrow twisting ridges,
Sharp-topped and jagged as a broken crosscut saw
Across the roof of all the Elk-world
On one ancient wandering trail,
Cutting crazily over rocks and dust and snow—
Gently slanting through high meadows,
Rich with scent of Lupine,
Rich with smell of Elk-dung,
Rich with scent of short-lived

Dainty alpine flowers.
And from the ridgetops I have followed you
Down through heather fields, through timber,
Downward winding to the hoof-churned shore of
One tiny blue-green mountain lake
Untouched by lips of men.

Ancient, wandering trails
Cut and edged by centuries of cloven hooves
Passing from one pasture to another—
Route and destination seeming aimless, but
Charted by the sharp-tempered guardian of creatures,
Instinct. A God coarse-haired, steel-muscled,
Thin-flanked and musky. Used to sleeping lonely
In the snow, or napping in the mountain grasses
On warm summer afternoons, high in the meadows.
And their God laughs low and often
At the man-made trails,
Precise-cut babies of the mountains
Ignorant of the fine, high-soaring ridges
And the slanting grassy meadows
Hanging over space—
Trails that follow streams and valleys
In well-marked switchbacks through the trees,
Newcomers to the Elk world.

(High above, the Elk walk in the evening
From one pasture to another
Scrambling on the rock and snow
While their ancient, wandering,
Aimless trails

And their ancient, coarse-haired,
Thin-flanked God
Laugh in silent wind-like chuckles
At man, and all his trails.)

Mt. St. Helens, Spirit Lake

"Out of the soil and rock"

Out of the soil and rock,
the growing season and spring, death
and winter,
out of the cold and rain, dust and sunshine,
came the music of cities and streets.
The people who take that music
                              into themselves,
creatures of salt, carbon, nitrogen, water,
may sometimes hang on the point of it,
hunger, an instant,
the world round the edge.

This city smoke and building steel
already is no more;
The music and cities of the future wait beyond the edge.

New York City

On the Doab of the Columbia and the Willamette

II

1949–1952

Lines on a Carp

old fat fish of everlasting life
in rank brown pools discarded by the river
soft round-mouth nudging mud
among the reeds, beside the railroad track

you will not hear the human cries
but pines will grow between those ties
before you turn your belly to the sun

A Sinecure for P. Whalen

Whalen, curious vulture,
Picked the Western mind,
Ate the cataracted eyes
That once saw Gwion race the hag
And addle gentlemen

Still unfilled, he skittered to
The sweet bamboo
Fed green on yellow silt
And built a poem to dead Li Po.
The Drunkard taught him how to dance,
Leave dead bodies to the plants,
Sleep out nights in rain.

For George Leigh-Mallory

Escaping Cambridge,
He turned away from London
With austere passion faced the seas.

Accompanied by numbered boxes
Crossed the plains in teeming summer
Soft eyes avoiding sores and hunger
And came to cool Darjeeling.

Hundreds of sleepy Sherpas
Hired at dawn, to carry
Tea and socks to Chomolungma.

Here, disregarding whimpered warnings
With practised skill maintained his life
In that translucent cold
And still had strength to breathe, and climb:

And found a hideous demon there
Waiting in a golden chair
With drums

This is what the simplest nomad knows.

Spring Songs

Out the building's shadow
A seagull bursts
Caught in slanted sunbeam,
Wing-slanted windward, head cocked sideways—
Eyeing the broil of cars
Within the shadow—

    what noise, what beasts rush
    on those ordered paths
    what ugly visions in this cubic tangle?

Early Spring afternoon. Befuddled bird,
Away!

Sky, high wind flowing
Hair, wind blown back
Water, black mud bank

Green growing
Wild things, free sowing
Wind-blown seed plants
Curl
Sprout
Tissue-tearing out

Message from Outside

I am the one who gnawed the blanket through
Peeped in the hole and saw with my left eye
The one-leg sliver man put out the fire.

I dug like mice below the cabin's floor
Crawling through oil and rotted hides, I broke
Into that curious handsewn box. Pursued by birds,
Threw my comb, my magic marbles to the wind,
Caught the last bus, and made it here on time.

Stop chewing gum, I show you what I stole—
Pine-marten furs, and box within each box,
The final box in swallow tendons tied,
Inside, an eye! It screws into
The center of your head.

But there they call me urine-boy,
And this deserted newsstand is quite safe.
Peer through this and watch the people spawn:
It makes me laugh, but Raven only croaks.

I saw Coyote! And I'll buy a gun,
Go back and build a monstrous general fire,
Watch the forests move into this town.

You stand cracking sunflower seeds and stare.

A Change of Straw

Flickering eye
Peers from a birdcage
        shivering lips of bone
        scratch, and a taste of shell

Feathers cram the mouth.
Birdtalk, loose claw curved
        on a stained bough
Slick eyes sleep
        in a dungheap

Ruffle of dusty wings.

Creep to the fence
Crisscross chickenwire screens at the sun
      crickets and plums
             wither dry

Caught in a barnyard!
        with a pocketful of straw.

Under the Skin of It

Naturally tender, flesh and such
Being entirely mortal, fragile
And complex as a model plane.
Demanding attention, in its unfair ways

Getting, of course, the pleasure that it seeks.

But is it pleased?
Flesh being a type of clay (or dust);
Spirit, the other, like a gas,
Rising and floating in the hollow
Of the Skull—

Which is to know the other's real delight?

Both under the skin, which stretches
As we grow, sagging a trifle
In the pinch of time. Enchanting
The thought of pleasure pleasing flesh and bone.

"dogs, sheep, cows, goats"

dogs, sheep, cows, goats
and sometimes deer, hear loud noises
crackling in bushes, and they flick
fly or creep, as rabbits do
does too, into warm nests. no talk
but chatters there, small throat sounds
ear-pricks, up or back. hooves
tinkle on creekbeds. who fears a talk-
less landscape, crowded with creatures
leaves. falls. undergrowth
crawls all night, and summer smells
deep in the bushes. crouch!
at the thorny stalks.

Birth of the Shaman

for Phil Whalen

  —well there he is. six a.m.
rhythmic flutter of the guts, now he's
born
in a drizzle of rain
  apple blossoms at Hood river,
smoke along water.
at river's mouth
tide frets the pilings.

  here he is.
back of the clearing, cedar drips.
clouds are breaking, Wy-east shines through
  —the white summit—
a truck honks, crossing the logging-road
in the valley.
  he is here.

Atthis

I.

The painful accumulation of our errors
In dry summer, and her loneliness
And that distracted weeping
Of hot endless afternoons
Foretold the famine

Her swimming fondness
Stretched taut in sterile time
Contracted into dusty fractions
And now the crops are failing.

Since my sorcery has failed
My blood must feed the soil.
Let no delirious priest proclaim
A second coming;
      these fragments will stay scattered.

2.

Her life blew through my body and away
I see it whirling now, across the stony places.

I lost her softly through my fingers,
Between my ribs in gentle gusts she
Sifted free, polishing the small bones.

The mute, thin framework takes the winds
That blow across the stony places.

3.

". . . Still, she reproached all lands,
calling them ungrateful
and unworthy of the gift of corn"

She shall not be mollified
Til men go mad, and trees have died
For no known reason on the heights
And cornfields withered overnight;
Til Elk have groaned with thirst
And flower buds refuse to burst
Til rivers turn the fish to stone
And rocks are heard again to moan:
Until the sun has been re-tied
To Machu Picchu, men who die
Will be but corpses dressed in frocks
Who cannot speak with birds or rocks.

4. TIGER SONG

I gnaw the body of delight
Spit the knotted gristle out
Lap the blood left lie by night

O see your joy digested here
Splintering to the bones of life
That torture with their fractured points
Your concupiscence into strife
Your love into a ball of hair
That cuts me worse than any knife

5.

Poorness and the pride we shared
Our mutual vicious natures bared
Made a jungle of a bed
Gnawed and comforted we fled.
It should have birthed a human child,
Instead our intellects ran wild.

My bitter foe, O sterile lover,
Stranded in my brain, you
Are loved, still loved, there
Which is nowhere, and leaves me
Strangled, bound and dangled, yet
Me, yet of most men most free.

6.

You've gone cold, I suppose
In the prosperous East, with a good job,
Your bright mind turned all brain,
Your wild dancing feet and eyes
Held still, fear
Finally running it all
Under some fancy name.
The summer I hitchhiked from New York
In the hottest week of August
Over the desert and into sea-fog
San Francisco and took you
From your Mother's place, and we hiked
Over Tamalpais, caught a ride
To Tomales Bay, and camped under pines.
You remember it now and put it down,
Turning hard. But I know
How clear and kind your love was
At eighteen, how keen your heart and eye,
How you wrote me of your downtown job,
Sandpipers at Stinson Beach, an old
German you met on a lonely hike
With freckles on his back—the sunburn
On your breasts. Even then
I had a terrible thought of time,
And age, and the death

Of our dream-like young love.
It began too soon,
Was too strong too soon,
And it's gone.

7.

Love me love, til trees fall flat
　　　　their trunks flail down the berries
Til ripe sharp vines crawl through the door
　　　　and the air is full of sparrows

I loved you love, in halls and homes
　　　　and through the long library;
I loved you in the pine and snow
　　　　now I love blackberry

8.

Half-known stars in the dawn sky
Purple Finch at the feed-tray
A broom beat on a back porch,
                         tea,
My bent legs, love of you.

9. UP THE DOSEWALLIPS

In the ruins of a CCC shelter
        cooking stew,
rain thru the broken shakes
gorge a low roar,
        rain and creeks—

A doe in the meadow
hair plastered to steaming flanks
        —hoofprints down gullies
wind whipping rain against cliffs

The trail fades in the meadow,
        cairns at each rise to the pass.
ash-scars, a ring of stone
        —we camped here one other summer—

rainsoaked and shivering
        kneedeep in squaw grass,

two days travel from roads.

Olympic Mountains

10. SEAMAN'S DITTY

I'm wondering where you are now
Married, or mad, or free:
Wherever you are you're likely glad,
But memory troubles me.

We could've had us children,
We could've had a home—
But you thought not, and I thought not,
And these nine years we roam.

Today I worked in the deep dark tanks,
And climbed out to watch the sea:
Gulls and salty waves pass by,
And mountains of Araby.

I've travelled the lonely oceans
And wandered the lonely towns.
I've learned a lot and lost a lot,
And proved the world was round.

Now if we'd stayed together,
There's much we'd never've known—
But dreary books and weary lands
Weigh on me like a stone.

Indian Ocean

The Broad Roads of the West

III

1952–1956

Bakers Cabin on Boone's Ferry Road

Frogs all night
    three white ducks
    chanting down the pond
    the yowling of the Siamese in heat
    the hot iron thud on spitting shirts
Dampish firewood squeaks and burns.
    four kittens and a baby squall
    in boxes by the kitchen stove.

Portland

Numerous Broken Eggs

Ejected from such pleasaunce,
Naturally some snivelling is expected.
Dalliance, in the old sense, these days rare;
One is not unaffected. Repair to symbols—
Fracture of the nerve. Keeping the word inflected
When monosyllabic pain would be the cure.

Nauseous, although inspired.
"Experience" had been the guide; freedom inflicted
By one's dismissal, proved to be the snare.
A dangling pink-eyed rodent could learn more
From such a death; retired for meditation
One sometimes wonders on the morpheme "pure."

In fact, the work was good.
When used the art is Art; dissected,
Each fragment starts anew, and resurrected,
A thousand baby starfish swarm the sea.
Perhaps not wisdom, but a certain gain—
Freedom is painless, pleasure not the lure.

And grammar is not the goal.
An insight into "structure" is the point—
Without a method—but a sudden stare
Refracted into objects, each Delight.

A junkyard neat as Nature, or a Bronze.
Unstuck from objects, meanings are unsure.

Gazing on unzoned stars the mind takes flight—
The Astrolabe precisely marks each place,
Moving on jewelled pinions, rimmed in brass
(Implicit order is the error here)
What fills the sky is keening of Swift wings!
All things seen by the naked eye, when closed.

The Lookouts

Perched on their bare and windy peaks
They twitter like birds across the fractured hills
Equipped by Science with the keenest tool—
A complex two-way radio, full of tubes.

The most alone, and highest in the land,
We trust their scrupulous vision to a man:
Assume their eyes are slitted to the sun
Searching each gorge and ridge-slope for a sign;

They are the ones to fix a point in sight
Reveal the azimuth of a distant flame,
Define the range and township of its light
And send us tramping blindly to the scene.

What we perceive on maps, in scale, is theirs:
Enormous and sprawling, falling on every side
Off to a rough horizon, scoured by ice,
Poking through clouds, and snowbound half the year.

Should we envy how they peer above
Over our rainy valleys, peak to peak,
Sending triumphant warnings out of space
That blare and startle, on the speaker box?

We need not listen. With a toggle switch
All that they say is stopped, our time is ours;
Or if that complex radio should break down—
Taught how to use, but not to fix, its tubes—

For all their artful watching, they are dumb.
Totally useless, lost to human speech,
They mutely have to make the long hike down.

History Must Have a Start

Upper Skagit country

Took all day to find it:
Mine cabin on Canyon Creek,
Looking for good tools, or an old brass
Safety razor with teeth.

Grown over with berries,
In a rubble of tailings,
Doorframe broke, roof sagged in,
Logs all skewed
About ready to fall.
Wheelbarrow, gears, a pick
Rusted by the door;
Inside, chairs broken, the mouse-proof
Chest filled with dry pellets and the
Shredded remains of a blanket.
Rusty crosscuts hung from the rafters.
Less than 20 years
Since the claim was abandoned,
But isolated: mice had moved in,
Plants poked through the puncheon.
Tools of our time, nothing for an
Archeologist, unless washboards are rare—

The whole works packed in on muleback
In pieces, and never enough gold to pay.

(No ceramics or statues
Like Harappa or Knossos,
These are from civilized times.)

Poem Left in Sourdough Mountain Lookout

I the poet Gary Snyder
Stayed six weeks in fifty-three
On this ridge and on this rock
& saw what every Lookout sees,
Saw these mountains shift about
& end up on the ocean floor
Saw the wind and waters break
The branched deer, the Eagle's eye,
& when pray tell, shall Lookouts die?

(A later lookout told me this poem was still pinned up in the cabin in 1968.)

Geological Meditation

Rocks suffer,
         slowly,
Twisting, splintering scree
Strata and vein
         writhe
Boiled, chilled, form to form,
Loosely hung over with
Slight weight of trees,
         quick creatures
Flickering, soil and water,
Alive on each other.

Matter
Bent into life,
Has hallucinations, astonished
Molecules informing in chains
         at last,
Incredible, the torture is known,
Called ideas.
         are they real?
Mountains are squashed like slugs.

Perception a chemical trick,
     dreams—
Men and beasts dream
Of pleasure.

Sourdough Mountain

Fording the Flooded Goldie River

Clamped to the log by the current
Stream breaking over my pack,
Fighting edging across,
Footholds wash out, felt
My body give way: to be
Swept beneath log and downstream,
Down the rocks, to the gorge.
Looked up from the rush of the torrent—
Sunlight in fir-boughs,
Midges in a sunpatch, a bird breaking up,
Cloud on the ridge,
Sky
Blue
I fought death:
    got across it
        alone.

Olympic Mountains

"Svāhā a Feminine Ending for Mantra"

Under the lilac, svāhā girl
eating the plum-pit, crunch.
bees buzz, green apples by watering holes
wet leaves and spiders in shadows.
green scum on the pond, beside
cement cisterns, moss green, what smells?
lift the rotted lid, smell it dark water.
they are breeding and feeding there
still water waits where, of a breeding day,
someone lets it out to seep
seep away.

"Wind has blown . . ."

Wind has blown
the blossoms down

no use dodging puddles
when your feet are soaked
       —scum of petals
slip on the wet walk;
a soft rain rides my skull.

I never loved you,
this spring or another.
rain in the plum bough

deer on the mountain
trout in the creek.

Berkeley

Song for a Cougar Hide

The Fully Human time is nigh,
Alas, the other beasts must die.

Sea lions beat and snort and dive.
Left no mottled fawn alive.
A black bear winters in his cave,
Coyote's bottled in his grave.

I have heard the fat buck snort
Gut-shot—winchester ninety-four
The Doe that winds a sitting sage,
Flees in such a fearful rage.

Wang Wei built his own Deer Park,
Chao-chou left no gate ajar
Murasaki rose at dawn and
Let the snow come blowing in.

I have logged and I have planted
Killed and birthed in measure
Forgot what I learned to learn
A cougar hide's my treasure.

(The cougar hide was carried off by an enterprising lad in San Francisco in 1970.)

"Plum petals falling . . ."

Plum petals falling
cherry still hard buds
drinking wine
in the garden
The landlady comes out
      in the twilight
and beats a rug.

The Rainy Season

Rain,
A steady drip from the eaves;
A trickle leaks down the wall,
Blankets piled in a dry corner
Wet jeans hang from the toe
               of a corkt boot
Perched on the redwood tokonoma.

Reading Rexroth's *Japanese Poems*.
The wet bike dries on the porch.
Walt Whitman, Hitomaro, Han Shan,
               here
In Berkeley December twentieth-
Century rain, in this city-
               world-war age,
And *of* it,
               the jazz of
Late nights streets and all these people
Springs from the same love
And cool eyes now
               as then.

Granite sierras, shelves of books,
Holy teachings, scatter
Aimlessly tumbling through
Years and countries—

Aristotle's herd of formal stars
                     stampedes—
The diamond-point mercy
Of this timeless rain.

The Genji Story

I once had a gray brindle tomcat named Genji
who would run off for days at a time
& come back to my pad & I'd feed him
    with horsemeat
& put medicine in his swoll eye.
His ears tattered up & his hide
    full of scratches
he'd sit on my lap while I read,
then he'd go through a gap in the window
& he made out much better than I.

I went off to a job in the mountains
and Genji got left with a friend
after a week Genji ran off
& was never seen ever again.
    that was some years ago,
at the moment I wonder
since I raised him from a kitten and fed him
    quite well,
if he's healthy & strong from the horsemeat
    we shared then
now living on scraps in wild streets
    where he dwells

Late October Camping in the Sawtooths

Sunlight climbs the snowpeak
     glowing pale red
Cold sinks into the gorge
     shadows merge.
Building a fire of pine twigs
     at the foot of a cliff,
Drinking hot tea from a tin cup
     in the chill air—
Pull on sweater and roll a smoke.
     a leaf
     beyond fire
Sparkles with nightfall frost.

Point Reyes

Sandpipers at the margin
        in the moon—
Bright fan of the flat creek
On dark sea sand,
        rock boom beyond:
The work of centuries and wars,
        a car,
Is parked a mile above
        where the dirt road ends.
In naked gritty sand,
Eye-stinging salty driftwood campfire
        smoke, out far,
It all begins again.
Sandpipers chasing the shiny surf
        in the moonlight—
By a fire at the beach.

April

I lay on my back
Watching the sun through the
Net glitter of your gold hair
Our naked selves on a
Steep grassy slope
Your third child in your belly
Your face by mine
Your husband's blessing
On our brief, doomed love
All of us in the heat of
April wine and sun
And sex and many friends
Our bodies flaring hot
Where we touch,
The sun burns the
Writhing snakebone
Of your back.

Makings

I watched my father's friends
Roll cigarettes, when I was young
Leaning against our black tarpaper shack.
The wheatstraw grimy in their hands
Talking of cars and tools and jobs
Everybody out of work.
   the quick flip back
And thin lick stick of the tongue,
And a twist, and a fingernail flare of match.
I watched and wished my overalls
Had hammer-slings like theirs.

The war and after the war
With jobs and money came,
My father lives in a big suburban home.
It seems like since the thirties
I'm the only one stayed poor.
It's good to sit in the
Window of my shack,
Roll tan wheatstraw and tobacco
Round and smoke.

Marin-an

Kyoto, and the Sappa Creek

IV

1956–1959

Longitude 170° West, Latitude 35° North

For Ruth Sasaki

This realm half sky half water,
  night black with white foam
  streaks of glowing fish
  the high half black too lit with
  dots of stars,
The thrum of the diesel engine twirling
  sixty-foot drive shafts of twin screws,
Shape of a boat, and floating
  over a mile of living seawater, underway,
  always westward, dropping
  land behind us to the east,
Brought only these brown Booby birds that trail
  a taste of landfall feathers in the craw
  hatchrock barrens—old migrations—
  flicking from off stern into thoughts,
Sailing jellyfish by day, phosphorescent
  light at night,
  shift of current on the ocean floor
  food chains climbing to the whale.

Ship hanging on this membrane infinitely
  tiny in the "heights" the "deep"
  air-bound beings in the realm of wind
  or water, holding hand to wing or fin
Swimming westward to the farther shore,
  this is what I wanted? so much

water in the world and so much crossing,
    oceans of truth and seas of doctrine
Salty real seas of our westering world,
    Dharma-spray of lonely slick on deck
Sleepy, between two lands, always a-
      floating world,
              I go below.

M.S. Arita Maru

For Example

There was an old Dutch lady
Lived in a room in the house
In front of my small shack
Who sat all day in the garden
By my door and read.
She said she knew the East
And once had seen a book
On Buddhist monks. "And you
Gott no business going to
Japan. The thing to be
Is life, is young and travel
Much and love. I know
The way you are, you study hard
But you have friends that
Come and stay, and bike, and
There's the little tree you
Planted by the wall" As I
Filled my water bucket from
A hose. The sun lit up
Her thin white hair a bird
Squawked from the Avocado at the air
& Bodhisattvas teach us everywhere.

Chion-In

Temple of the Pure Land

         hot blue
high clouds pile
flicker-eave pigeons under dark wood
clink bells and wood clack chant
         gold, wood, incense,
trees behind—
         stop here
on the granite step
foot-polished and eat a plum.

Bomb Test

The fish float belly-up, for real—
Uranium in the whites
                    of their eyes
They've been swimming
Deep down where it's black when a
Silvery snow of something queer
                    glinted in
From cirrus clouds to the seamounts,
Through all the food chains,
Shrimp to tuna, the currents,
Riding the waves.

Kyoto

Dullness in February: Japan

The high-class families
Teach their virgin daughters
English, flowers, and Tea:
Culture of the East—poor girls
Ride boys' bikes balancing noodles.

Brutal sergeants, vicious aesthetes,
    the meeting
Of the worst of East and West.
Silly priests in temples
Far too fine for now.
Discipline for what end?
We gave up wisdom long ago,
Enlightenment is kicks
    —but there is better.
Cold smooth wood floors
And doves, stone pools, moss
Under maples, silent frosty rooftiles
Slanting high—what sense
The old boys made—
Confucius, Lao-tzu, Tu Fu, Sesshu
    and the rest,
Through the centuries, peed off
By politicians in their robes.
Perhaps some flame remains.
    I hope

Again some day
To hit the night road in America
Hitchhiking through dark towns
Rucksack on my back,
To the home of a
Poverty-stricken witty
Drunkard friend.

Map

A hill, a farm,
A forest, and a valley.
Half a hill plowed, half woods.
A forest valley and a valley field.

Sun passes over;
Two solstices a year
Cow in the pasture
Sometimes deer

A farmhouse built of wood.
A forest built on bones.
The high field, hawks
The low field, crows

Wren in the brambles
Frogs in the creek
Hot in summer
Cold in snow

The woods fade and pass.
The farm goes on.
The farm quits and fails
The woods creep down

Stocks fall you can't sell corn
Big frost and tree-mice starve
Who wins who cares?
The woods have time.
The farmer has heirs.

The Feathered Robe

For Yaeko Nakamura

On a clear spring windless day
Sea calm, the mountains
        sharp against the sky,
An old man stopped in a sandy
        seashore pine grove,
Lost in the still clear beauty.
Tracing a delicate scent
        he found a splendid robe
Of feathers hanging on a bough.

        Robe over his arm
        He heard   alarm
        Stop, and there he saw
        A shining Lady,
                naked from her swim.

        Without my feathered robe
        that useless-to-you a human,
        Robe, I cannot,
        Home, I
        Cannot fly,
                        she cried

And for a dance
        he gave it back.
A dance,

she wore it glinting in the sun
Pine shadow breeze
Fluttering light sleeves—

　　　old man watching saw
　　　all he dreamed in youth
　　　the endless springtime
　　　morning beauty
　　　of the world
　　　　　　as

She, dancing, rose
Slow floating over pines
High beyond the hills
　　　　　　a golden speck
In blue sky haze.

　　Nō play "Hagoromo"

On Vulture Peak

All the boys are gathered there
Vulture Peak, in the thin air
Watching cycles pass around
From brain to stone and flesh to ground,
Where love and wisdom are the same
But split like light to make the scene,
Ten million camped in a one-room shack
Tracing all the causes back
To Nothing which is not the start
(Now we love, but   here we part)
And not a one can answer why
To the simple garden in my eye.

I.
J.K. & me was squatting naked and sandy
At McClure Beach steaming mussels, eating,
Tossing the shells over our shoulders,
A pair of drunk Siwash starting a shellmound.
Neuri sleeping off a hangover face down
At the foot of a cliff; sea lions off shore

II.
Are bums and drunks truly Angels?
Hairy Immortals drinking poorboys in doorways?
Poor Abelard, thou'rt clipped!
                    the vomit

& prickles of a gritty desert drug
    sweat and fire
Berry lather & lapping dogs—
    All babies
Are unborn; tracking the moon through
Flying fenceposts a carload of groceries, home—
What home, pull in park at, and be known?

III.
    "the little cloud"
A nebula seen slantwise by the naked eye.
The curse of man's humanity to man. "My hair
  is in a pony-tail, I run!"
Each day a lunchpail and a shirtful of sawdust.
Old women dry pods fry corn in the cinders.
The head is a hawk on a boulder
The boulder a nest of coiled snakes

IV.
Nearer than breathing
Closer than skin
    smack in the earballs
nosehalls, brainpans, tongueclucks
eyeholes, prickbones,
answer! answer! why!
   "with lowered lids
   i have entered
     nibbana"

V.
Wisdom of the Arab:
   a camel lets her milk down
when tickled in the snatch.

philosophers are horrified
because there is no cause
because everything exists
because the world is real and so are they
and so is nothing is, not nothing save us—
                    bony jungle spring
                         Shakya in the boondocks.
          a broken start,
                         sprout,
                    is REALLY gone
                                        wow, he
always been standin there
                    sweatin' and explainin'?

VI.
          gone where.
Nowhere, where he came from
          thus that thing
          that thus thing
                         where were you born from
                         born from, born from—
Did you fall   fall   fall
                                   fall
          from the salmonberry bough?
Are you the reborn soul
          of a bitter cheated chief?
                              —I came out my mammy
Slick & yapping like a seal
My uncle washed me in the brine
I was a hero & a hunter in my time
A badger gave me visions
A whale made me pure

I sold my wife & children
& jumped into a mirror

VII.

Hot wispy ghosts blown
            down halls between births,
                    hobo-jungles of the void—
—Where did we meet last? where
Were you born? Wobblies of the Six
Realms—huddling by some campfire
                                in the stars
Resting & muttering before a birth
On Mars,

VIII.

What can be said about a Rabbit
Solitary and without context
Set before the mind. Was it born?
Has it horns? Dream people walking around
In dream town
            —the city of the Gandharvas—
        not a real city, only the
                        memory of a city—
"The mind dances like the dancer
The intellect's the jester
The senses seem to think the world's a stage—"

IX.

For forty years the Buddha begged his bread
And all those years said nothing, so he said,
& Vulture Peak is silent as a tomb.

The Bodhisattvas

Some clap hands, some throw flowers,
Pat bread, lie down, sell books,
Do quaint dance steps, jingling jewels,
Plant wild Thyme in engine-blocks,
Make dark grimace stroking mules,
Fall backward into tom-tom thumps;
& cheer and wave and levitate
And pass out lunch on Vulture Peak
Enlightening gardens, parks, & pools.

A Monument on Okinawa

"One hundred twenty schoolgirls
Committed suicide together here."
Dead now thirteen years.
Those knot-hearted little adolescents
In their fool purity
Died with a perverse sort of grace;
Their sisters who lived
Can be seen in the bars—
The agreeable hustlers of peace.

Straits of Malacca 24 oct 1957

a.

    Soft rain on the
gray ocean, a tern
still glides low over
whitecaps
after the ship is gone

b.

    Soft rain on

                .gray sea

a tern

       glides brushing

                waves

    The ship's silent

            wake

c.   *Fog of rain on*

          water

    Tern glides
    Over waves,

         the

     wake

The Engine Room, S.S. Sappa Creek

Cool northern waters
Walk around the engine room where
Seven months I worked.

Changing colors
Like seasons in the woods
One week the rails and catwalks all turned red
Valve wheels grow green
Fade with soot and oil,
And bloom again bright yellow after weeks

Paintbrush, pots, & walking round.
The overhead line
Big enough to crawl through
       like I did in Ras Tanura,
Three months ago was white. & now it's
Gray.
Under rusty floorplates
       bilges lap
Venture there in slop of oil & brine
To clean out filters in the fuel oil line.

The engineer said
Paint the hot-lines silver.
I stood on ladders with a silver brush.
Skittering gauges tacked up everywhere

Pressure, pressure on each pump and pipe;
Heat of the steam, heat of the oil,
Heat of the very water where we float
Wrote down in the log book every hour,

Boilers, turbines, nest of bulkheads,
Hatches, doorways, down & sidewise, up,
But no way out.
Sweeping & changing all of it by bits.
—A yard of pipe replaced
A bearing in the trash can.
Me changing less by far—

All that time
Chipping, painting, fixing, this machine.
Lugging wrenches take off manhole covers
Polish tubes, and weld and gasket
            til the damn thing goes,

On land nobody off this ship
Will ever be so free or gay
Though in San Pedro we will
            each man get paid off about
                three thousand dollars cash
In two more days.

Hills of Home

I.
Today is like no day that
came before
I'll walk the roads and trails to Tamalpais.
    one clear day of fall,
    wind from the north
    that cleans the air a hundred
       miles

A little girl in a dark garage:
her home in the redwood shade,
     her father there
     he saws
   a board
(across the hill is
    nothing but sunshine,
liveoak, hardscrabble, hot little
      lizards)
       wet shade
made those huge damp trees.
At my sister's house
at the foot of the trail,
I stop
drink coffee, tell her of my walk.

II.

I know nothing
of planes: I have seen pictures
        of the bomb:
It is beautiful to watch
jets skim by Richmond
        and the prison, pass the
        mountain, out
on a shining endless ocean
lift up on clouds and gleam
        even the noise is
interesting to hear and how it
        echoes across these
        manzanita hills.

III.

Stop the sailing sailboats:
        they are still.
just west of Alcatraz,
beyond them San Francisco town
        bonewhite in blue sea bay
        two major jails
        an oil refinery
sailboats all the way.
I eat my lunch on
sharp rocks at the top.

IV.

to see your own tracks climbing
up the trail that you go down.
the ocean's edge is high
it seems to rise and hang there
halfway up the sky.

V.

sun goes down.
on the dark side of the hill
        through pecker redwood trees
        in gloom and chill
        a small red blossom
        agitates the shade.
                the pipeline trail.
weave forward
carried on these feet
feel of the body
& abstract recollection held in time.
abandoned house at road's end:
        gray and real the
        glassless square holes
black/the steps all sidewise
and the wise inside.

I walk back to my cabin door
And leave this day behind.

The North Coast

Those picnics covered with sand
No money made them more gay
We passed over hills in the night
And walked along beaches by day.

Sage in the rain, or the sand
Spattered by new-falling rain.
That ocean was too cold to swim
But we did it again and again

The Wide Pacific

V

1959–1969

One Year

The hills behind
        Santa Barbara
           from the sea.
Pedro at midnight.
        three thousand dollars
Cash in hundred dollar bills
      —the Wakayama hills—
        each time
A ship hits land the land
      is new.
April. Oakland at eight A.M.
        hotcakes in San Francisco, ten
(Pago a month gone by)
      —jukebox tunes in
         far-off foreign towns;
Mt. Hiei. Tamalpais.
      June. The Desolation
        Valley snow.
She read her poems.
      Sierras in August, always
"Will I ever see those hills again?"
      rain. lightning
        on Whitney
Crackling hair on end.
      Once
        on the coast,

I heard of "Sticky Monkey Flower"
            "It makes you high"
Seals laugh
            in the seaweed—
The mind aches
            seeing a tanker passing
                out at sea.
At Port Townsend on the Sound
            I didn't stop
                to see Aunt Minnie:
Who gave cookies to my father
            1910. On Mt. St. Helens
Rotten glaciers turned us back.
            Hitching home,
                a German boy from BC
In one sweep drove me down.
                Columbus Street San Francisco
The bed falls on the floor.
            months of Marin-an
Learning again the names of birds & trees;
I saw the sea
            from Santa Barbara,
January. The water always warm.
            Big Sur in the fog;
In February packed my sleeping bag.
            Piers, blast
                whistle & the ship
Backs back & all
            we never stop to do
                & think of then
Can cry—lightship, albatross,
            the ocean like a friend,
Yokohama, Fuji, where its always been—

Mt. Hiei. On the river.
        settled here.
Today, America, Japan,
        one year.

Housecleaning in Kyoto

This red washrag
        full of holes
faded grayish-pink
from scouring smoky
pots—before I throw it out,
        we found it:
camping
Potrero Meadows 1956

(Jack Kerouac and I took a three day hike on the far slopes of Tamalpais just before I left for Asia—the washrag salvaged there got somehow to Japan.)

Seeing the Ox

Brown ox
Nose snubbed up
Locking his big head high
    against telephone pole
    right by Daitoku   temple—
Slobbering, watching kids play
    with rolling eye,

Fresh dung pile under his
    own hind hooves.

Kyoto

After the Typhoon

Rain whipped up the umbrella
The river was boiling down trees.
I stood on the bridge in a puddle
And crossed to the Yase zoo.
Three monkeys on top of a rock
Made a house for the new baby,
Hawk plucking a soggy old fish—
And the bear asleep: a brown muzzle
Deep in a damp cement cave.

Three Poems for Joanne

I. LOVING WORDS

Her big basket
                blonde hair drawn back
                over the ears
a directoire, or jacobean feel
                last summer, on crutches
hobbling down the steep hill trail.
sitting beside the geraniums
marking the eucalyptus rustle—sea wind—
                                        listening
i was chopping wood around the corner
down the hill.
                        axe-sound
                        the bird
                        the wind
            the snorting horses & the starting cars,

loving words—
            "be true
to the *poem*"
nothing will shake that
                fine commitment down.

2. THE HEART OF THE WOOD

The cool
     clearing.
We have never seen
Such trees or
        flowers.
We are bare
In the open.
       here make
       our love
No one will
Watch us.
This place is
  Too far
In.

3. JOANNE MY WIFE

Joanne my wife
why frown
long legs are lovely
         I like yr
         freckld breast
         you butt me at night
              asleep
cry out for mother
hurt wild
like child
in dreams
         I cd write you
      no "love" poem
             so long.

    fights and the frown
             at dawn.

Tenjin

We had ten Zen monks
            down for lunch—
"tenjin" the head monk said:
in China it was just a bun ("t'ien-hsin")
means "that the heart"
it means a real feed
            in Japan today.
"they still have buns in China
called 't'ien-hsin'"—
Dimsum, in Cantonese.

Joanne, Aronowitz, and I
once had tenjin (dim-sum)
on a quiet San Francisco
Sunday morning, chinatown.

Parting with Claude Dalenberg

Why don't we get drunk
      sit all night facing the moon
  "opening our hearts"
        as men did long ago?

last night was full moon, but
              too cloudy.
one bottle of saké
        soon gone.
at lunchtime today you stopped by
your ship sails from Kobe at six.

eight years: San Francisco, the
beaches, the mountains,
           Japan.

Quiet talk and slow easy pace.
with your rucksack to India,
Europe, return

ease of the world, the light
          rain

as though we might
somewhere be
          parting again.

          Kyoto

Crash

An old man riding his slow bike
Right down the center of the gravel road
At walking pace to talk to two old women
Bundled firewood balanced on their heads,
Distracted or intense in other mind
I picked the space between him and the two
Without a horn-honk tried to ride
Straight through, he swerved inside,
We soft collided in slow motion,
Motorcycle, man, and bike.
In grooved and rutted gravel powder dirt.
He red-faced cursed me in the local way
As I responded in a fair polite
Level of language, Ohara busses,
Waiting at our rear,
The peasant women waited down the road.
My fault. And he recalled he knew my face
And house, a Yase dweller too,
He said he would be madder,
But knew me now. It was not real
Even while kicking back the crash-bars into line.
Where was my mind.
Hieizan over, and the stream,
And all the cherry trees around
About to bloom—and us not hurt—
He rode away, his old brown overcoat

And rubber work shoes puffing dirt.
I overtook him. Later at the temple
My hands began to tremble:
I saw my inattention,
Tiny moment in the thread,
Was where the whole world could have turned
And gone another way.

Kyoto

Two Comments

I.
I walk the oldest culture on earth & hold
concrete & asphalt concordances.
childhood of flush and propellor
always a bored eye on the factories
I tell you shoes
what can I elaborate of doorknob?
privacy always.
your railway timetable spells.
we were raised in a warehouse
& teach the archaic
way of Technique.
   I know the whole of my time.
my people half-lidded drive their machines
what other people from birth
    have known orgies and tigers?
        my heart?

II.
Kennedy, Krushchev, & Nixon
your little children will all be destroyed
& the potsherds heap over them
nobody follows the
Logic of this to its end.

"Riding the hot electric train"

Riding the hot electric train
Between temples and companies,
Trading my mother tongue
For the means to stay here,

I know what
Dante meant
Entering that cave
In a forest when faced by wolves.

I must not keep forgetting
I am still travelling
The land between here
And the sea.

The man on the mountain is wise,
In town he is
Jackrolled and
Gets clap from good-hearted whores.

Foreigners

tall
yellow teeth
deep voices
pimples.
walk like policemen
hands in their pockets,
always wanting girls.
music hard and fast
getting drunk
fighting with their fists

laughing at each other.
their eyes
aren't really blue.

Kyoto Vacation

Down from the country, old train bogies,
Piled up with plaid country quilt
They've been travelling days,
Purple flag says "Hokkaido"
Lined up on the platform in groups
Loads wrapped in furoshikis,
Red-faced geezer with white fringe-beard
All dowdy, shabby,
From cold pebble saltshore towns
And sugarbeet fields.
This is their Kyoto
          (who's that foreigner—)
Busy, with someplace to go.
Teapots and bedding,
A bunch of old lambs in their huddles
They get told where to go and have fun—

This Is Living

Who's that old lady?
She's going to get her
Nice kimono all dirty
Being sick
In the station
Of the train

In Tokyo: At Loose Ends

all those books and those clothes
        are forgotten.
how could we have cared.
those plans, those evenings
        all over.
the whole world is here—
paste in the postoffice,
        paintings in museums
people in houses,
        me on my feet through the town.
liking it,
        ready to leave.

English Lessons at the Boiler Company

The western hills curve down from Mt. Atago
Toward Osaka plains and the inland sea.
Sun, snow, clouds, flurry and glitter,

From long high sheds comes the rivetting,
Shriek of steam pressure tests,
They make boilers—

File into the small, heated, carpetted,
Office room: start teaching language,
Strange feeling sounds, odd puffs and buzzes,
Bend tongues, re-wrap the brain,

Over the plains,   snow-whirling clouds.

From Below

turkey buzzards wheeling
          wheeling

quivering inter-crossing
          zag   fern fronds

high blue two
     supersonic feathery ice-
          tracks sail south

rear jet trail plumes crossing
          with the leader

sun flashes the buzzard breast
          over shingle corners
          this old redwood house.

The Fruit

More sour, more bitter than lemon
It had seemed a sweet coarse orange,

Even bananas with seeds.
Huge blooms of no odor

Brook water warm to the touch.
Dreaming but not quite sleeping,
Wakened but not awake.

The Ride

To
Force to the furthest edge where
　　it still holds up

Riding Visions isn't fun
　　must be done.

Only
When children and friends
All in a whirl go wild for a while—
Lips drawing over our mouths—hair in our eyes—
　　can we rest and smile.

Riding the edge makes one crude.
The Chinese poets
　　I have no heart to read.

We trap dreams
And club them,
Skin them out, tools are few,
The guts and the shit can be used—
To keep up this work
　　poison is food.

To draw the times over the edge
To go where we could.

Then

When everybody in the world has a car
and nobody knows the smell
people will be amazed at our carpentry
all the deer in zoos
they'll remember wild animals and trees
call their housecats "tiger"
dream of the days
when men were poor and dirty—
it was great—
beggars, the wine-red saris
of outcaste Indian girls
lean hunger in the rain
—we were
alive, then

Saying Farewell at the Monastery after Hearing the Old Master Lecture on "Return to the Source"

At the last turn in the path
     "goodbye—"
     —bending, bowing,
    (moss and a bit of
       wild
         bird–)
down.

Daitoku-ji Monastery

Farewell to Burning Island

A white bird lands on the ship
—The smoking island from afar
Feet scorch on the white deck
—Sailing east across the ocean
Once more.

Suwa-no-se Island, East China Sea

Shasta Nation

VI

1968–1985

First Landfall on Turtle Island

Crossing eastward the Pacific on the Washington Bear
The high route, just under the Aleutians
Twelve days storms and heavy seas
Kai laughs in his playpen hanging on
Rough or gentle weather, it's all one to him—
Masa seasick, naps in the daytime,
Last morning early: blue and smooth.
Watch for Gray Whales from the flying deck
A whale blows over by the lightship
    brisk winds, Ah, Ah,
Masa in her yellow parka, "the SKIN
    of the California hills!"
Seagull sails in, hangs there, a yard off my eye
Past the port side the flash of the Point Reyes lighthouse—
A whale rolls up, doesn't blow, just by the ship.

The long dawn chilly curve blue-purple,
    that's Bolinas, that's the oak in the
    meadow on the ridge under Tam
    I sat with Lew at—

A long land, a smooth land, clear sky,
    a whale,
    a gull,
To say hello.

Alabaster

The leather fringes
    swing on the thighs.
    ah   so hot
    only beads to wear are cool

And the girls chests like the mens
    are bare
    in the shade
    but the girls differ though the men are same.

Tanya's bosom like a drawn bow
    Holly like a load of flowers
    Ann's gracious fruits
    Masa brown and slimming down
        from milky dark-veined weight
    and, slighter than the rest,

But strongly dappled in the
    sweltering-shady mind,
    Edie's alabaster breasts.

For the women carpenters of Kitkitdizze

The Years

The years seem to tumble
    faster and faster
    I work harder
    the boys get larger
    planting apple and cherry.

In summer barefoot,
    in winter rubber boots.

Little boys bodies
    soft bellies, tiny nipples,
    dirty hands

New grass coming
    through oakleaf and pine needle
    we'll plant a few more trees
    and watch the night sky turn.

Burned Out

An ancient incense cedar stump to burn
Against which piled the limbs
Of gnarly wolf-tree pine
Those limbs that burn black smoke
And dripping pitch
Along with other trunks and twigs
And heaps of manzanita, set fire to,
In February on a day when rain
Will just start after nine dry days.
Brush pile burning is a time to sit
Or nap by the big fire glow
Then pile on more
Dragged out from toppled beetle-kills.
Next day it rained some lightly
Then all night rain and wind that woke us
Heavy rain lashes and cascades
On the buddha-like seven-ton tile roof
And stout pine-pillared body of our *kum*,
Even after rain
The cedar stump still flickering in the wind
Smoking through the storm
Turned to a hole in the ground,
Black lips hissing jets of steam
From white ash mounds
Fire reaching deeper to its end
In narrow pitchy roots

It arrives at the beginning
Where a cone-flaked seed
Made its sprout.
Leaves a ghost-root hole,
A perfect cast of what's below,
So above. Cool.
Burned out. Again.

O

For Ed Schafer

O
Mistress of Bobcats
Lady of Sagebrush
      why do you fool me?
      showing me
              you
In a thousand shapes.
Groin, eyes, flank, toes,
Arches,
Lifts of the arm,
Hollow soft of the back of the knees,

      sweets and salts of
      lips and gulfs,
      halls of deep flesh song—
Why do you trick me
Queen of Taste?
      whose real beauty

      is none.

To Meet with Agaricus Augustus

Back up the ridge
at Bloody Run
is an old time sawmill
fifty years gone,

At Bloody Run
in the sawmill ruin
we found a mushroom
one foot wide.

I felt small.
To see that one,
So rare and great,
and good to eat,

"The Prince"

Too Many Chickens Gone

Bobcat paws. Bobcat pelt
   bobcat bobtail tail-bone;
      tufted ears.
Glazed eyes   heaving belly
    kicking chicken-dusty
      dirt

wire fencing fenced him in
his fur in puffs on wire
where up he jumped,
    and fell.

For Alan Watts

He blazed out a new path for all of us
And came back and made it clear.
Explored the side canyons and deer trails
And investigated cliffs and thickets.
Many guides would have us travel
Single file, like mules in a pack-train;
And never leave the trail.
Alan taught us to move forward like the breeze;
Tasting the berries—greeting the bluejays—
Learning and loving the whole terrain.

on his death

Original Vow

pollen, eagle down
light-on-the-water
bird-rising

    rattlesnake nose-pits
sense heat
      "See" the heart in a
          mouse
            beating;
    strike for the meat.

No Shoes No Shirt No Service

Padding down the street, the
Bushmen, the Paiute, the Cintas Largas
    are refused.
The queens of Crete,
The waiting-ladies of the King of Bundelkhand.
Tārā is kept out,
Bare-breasted on her lotus throne.

    (officially, no one goes through
    unofficially, horses go through,
    carriages go through—)

The barefoot shepherds, the bare-chested warriors

    (what is this gate,
    wide as a highway
    that only mice can enter?)

The cow passed through the window nicely—
Only the tail got stuck,

And the soils of this region will be fertile again
After another round of volcanoes
Nutrient ash—
    Shiva's dancing feet
    (No shoes)

Kine

Eight cows
        on a hillside
One stands,
        the brown
Grass around them flattened down.
Cows rest
        nestled on jut of hip
        springy rib and skin,
A huge taut sigh
        from the road,
        passing by

"The Trail Is Not a Trail"

I drove down the Freeway
And turned off at an exit
And went along a highway
Til it came to a sideroad
Drove up the sideroad
Til it turned to a dirt road
Full of bumps, and stopped.
Walked up a trail
But the trail got rough
And it faded away—
Out in the open,
Everywhere to go.

Poetry Is the Eagle of Experience

All the little mice of writing letters,
Sorting papers,
And the rabbits of getting in the wood,
The big Buck of a lecture in town.

Then, walk back into the brush
To keep clearing a trail.
High over even that,
A whistle of wings!
Breath of a song.

Calcium

The doe munches on rotten cow-skull
bone, she is pregnant.
Back of the woodshed
hooves rustling dry poison oak.

Cement hardens up at the footings
poured for the barn.

Molecule by molecule
drawn in and saved by
single swimming cells,
a few sparks of Calcium
like Blue Whales
far apart, and streaming through the sea.

High Quality Information

A life spent seeking it
Like a worm in the earth,
Like a hawk. Catching threads
Sketching bones
Guessing where the road goes.
Lao-tzu says
To forget what you knew is best.
That's what I want:
To get these sights down,
Clear, right to the place
Where they fade
Back into the mind of my times.
The same old circuitry
But some paths color-coded
Empty
And we're free to go.

The Arts Council Meets in Eureka

We held a meeting in Eureka
    far in the corner of the state.
    some flew, but I drove it straight—
    east beside Clear Lake
    through level valleys first,
    then chaparral,
    until we reach the cooler coastal air
    and camped the first night under
    tanbark oak.

Next day saw the tallest tree of all:
clapped our hands and asked for longer life.

Eureka by the bay:
    a nuclear power plant; heaps of chips.
    the sawmills owned by men from far away,
    the heaped up kerf
    of mountainsides of logs.
    stand at the edge of sea air fog,

No one who lives here
    has the power
    to run this town.

Ordering Chile Verde in Gallup

Wet lips sidewise,
lightly chewing gum,
half parted, combed out bangs
earrings almost to the shoulder
calm wide eyes,
large soft
wide-moving body swinging
out-pointed breasts
in her white waitress dress,
she tosses head and
calls back to the kitchen,

"Green, with"

Getting There

Padma Sambhava, the furry tail
Lin-chi, tooth and claws
Buddha-nature, smoke blown through passes
Ezra Pound, the purple-white Jimson Weed
            trumpet flower.

Lion roar splitting dumb ears.

The turned up oak-leaf duff scoop
Left hollow, empty, damp, where a doe
            found out and ate a mushroom.
Snowflakes settle in on coiling millipede
At edge of rotten pine.

The summit of the world.
We were always climbing,
Sometimes resting,
Stopping to talk or to take a drink—

The summit always there.
How many steps, how many bows,
Deep sighs, sturdy frowns,
Brothers and sisters all the way:
            no matter who goes or who stays.

Sustained Yield

For the treeplanters

Spain, Italy, Albania, Turkey, Greece,
once had hills of
oak and pine

This summer-dry winter-wet
            California
manzanita, valley oak, redwood,
            sugar pine, our folk
sun, air, water,
            our toil,

Topsoil, leafmold, sifted dirt,
hole-in-the-ground

Hold the whip of a tree
steady and roots right
somebody tamp the
            earth, as it's slipped in,
down.

Keep trees growing in this
            Shasta nation alta California
            Turtle island
ground.

"Low winter sun . . ."

Low winter sun. Kai sits on the *engawa*
reading, next to him Ediza—and steady
drips off the eaves, of melting snow.
He looks, she looks,
          through a veil of waterdrops
off the edge of the eaves—snow melts
     in the warm brief winter sun slant—
          he's reading; at me

lunch pail in hand down the path.
     Him ten,
               cat six,
                    me forty-eight.

The Weave

Walking the Yuba canyon
    through buckbrush, berberia,
    water-curling wilderness

    all the lines sending
    realms overlapping

Human projects break their weave.
    they re-group
    knitting and probing,
    don't miss a beat.

Hear, walking the wilderness
    steady rivers hissing over boulders
    Nuthatch, Peewee,
        peeeeeeeeeeee

Enforcement

Low planes—
>   the government has eyes
>   in the sky.

Fast cars—
>   the county police
>   are on the dirt roads.

When the people were poor
>   they were left alone

Now, with more money,
>   the police and the thieves
>   both come for the crop.

Yuba Country Autumn

Today is the first day of autumn
    long shadows—cool wind—

A squirrel scolds and chatters
    from up in a pine at the cat.
    chickens out of the coop
    scratching dry leaves,

A government plane breaks the quiet.
    flies over the treetops
    searching again,

So many arrested
    for growing some plants.
    A hard winter coming
    for the back-country families;

    the squirrel scolds and chatters
A big green acorn,
    whack! on the woodshed roof.

The Spirits Wait and Sing
Beneath the Land

"Lassen's one big sweat lodge"

Under the hills the *Kukini* gamble
      hand-games, marked bones
      whose bones?
      waiting

Land tilting, streams cutting,
The People, to change,
      Kukini gamble,
      who'll win?
Will the People
      come back again?

A mountain like a sweat lodge
Smoke Hole smoking
Red rock running
Rivers flapping off in steam.

Bear

Kai was alone by the pond in the dusk. He heard
    a grunt and felt, he said, his hair tingle.
    He jumped on a bike and high-tailed it down
    the trail, to some friends.

Scott stood alone in the dark by the window. Clicked
    on his flashlight and there out the window, six
    inches away, were the eyes of the bear.

Stefanie found her summer kitchen all torn up.

I went down the hill to the beehives next morning—
    the supers were off and destroyed, chewed comb
    all around, the whole thing tipped over, no
    honey, no larvae, no bees,

But somewhere, a bear.

Arktos

(Pythagoras: She-bears are the hands of Rhea)

Sighing, bursting: steam—sulfur—lava—
Rolling and bubbling up, falls out,
Back in on itself
        curling and licking
           getting hard.

Lichens, oak groves, float in up like cloud shadows
Soft, soft,
Loving plant hands.

Tendrils slip through til they meet
        it pulls taut
Green and quick—sap call swells the hills

        changing cloud mountain
        changing cloud gate

Rainbow glimmering with swallows, looping cranes.

        icefields and snowfields ring
        as she comes
        gliding down the rainbow bridge

        Joy of the Mountains
        "The Great She Bear"

Fear Not

Will Dallas grow, or wither?
   said the paper.
"Let the bastards freeze in the dark."

     dead or alive?
     knocking at the stone door.
"Goat ropers need love too."
     embracing more than "being"
     the stone door knocks back.

Two women masturbate a corpse,
                   in clay,
One holds his chin—

The Fox-girls switch from
     human to fox-form
     right during the party!
        one man
who was doing cunnilingus on his friend,
     now finds a mouth
     of fur.
The saké bottles clatter down.

and daylight; all's well,
just a little sore—

Who's there?
No one who

I See Old Friend Dan Ellsberg on TV in a Mountain Village of Japan

His familiar youthful face
    as I stand with my back
    to the open-door dark
    looking into the TV light,

In the Yura valley, Honshu,
    ricefields and cedars,
    an owl calls
    in from the night.

Dan's message is good,
    stop arming, put the missiles away,
    Japan shouldn't join in.
    the owls hoot again,
    The whole nation of owls
    In all the dark trees
    calls in and agrees.

Waikiki

For Chris Pearce

A steep reef of concrete, steel, and glass
Owned by one man forty percent
Whose ex-lover watches the scene for him
While tending a classy bar,
And white people get a touch of symbolic brown
   at the shore,
Brown people get their symbolic touch of white,

Twenty-five thousand rooms, on a swamp.
In the heart of it all a Banyan:
Arching and spreading,
   surrounded by buildings,
Is the god of the place. Is a ghost of the past,
The life of the present,
   the hope of the future.
(A fortune-teller booth
   tucked away in a nook in the roots.)

"She dreamed . . ."

She dreamed she was a cougar,
    a panther,
    A great cat bounding,
    and she is.
    Young, slim, nullipara,
    a wild cat like that
    in the dark, in the night.
Feeling the whap of the forepaw,
Making the turn,
    springing aside—right—left—
    bounding and curving.
Long loins stretched out behind.
Graceful tail arching and following
As she told it—
    as we walked on a dark
    mountain road.

Her eyes laughed as she danced how she
    leaped in the dream
    as she showed me,

Later, and back under a shelter
We curled up in a corner
I kissed her small nipples
    and bit her a little, and we
    growled and purred.

We Make Our Vows
Together with All Beings

Eating a sandwich
At work in the woods,

As a doe nibbles buckbrush in snow
Watching each other,
chewing together.

A Bomber from Beale
over the clouds,
Fills the sky with a roar.

She lifts head, listens,
Waits til the sound has gone by.

So do I.

At White River Roadhouse
in the Yukon

For Gary Holthaus

At White River Roadhouse in the Yukon
A bell rings in the late night:
A lone car on the Alaska highway
Hoping to buy gas at the shut roadhouse.

For a traveller sleeping in a little room
The bell ring is a temple in Japan,
In dream I put on robes and sandals
Chant sūtras in the chilly Buddha-hall.

Ten thousand miles of White Spruce taiga.
The roadhouse master wakes to the night bell
Enters the dark of ice and stars,
To sell the car some gas.

The Persimmons

In a cove reaching back between ridges
the persimmon groves:
leaves rust-red in October
ochre and bronze
scattering down from the
hard slender limbs of this
slow-growing hardwood
that takes so much nitrogen
and seven years to bear,
and plenty of water all summer
to be bearing so much and so well
as these groves are this autumn.
Gathered in yard-wide baskets
of loose open weave
with mounds of persimmons just picked
still piled on the ground.
On tricycle trucks
pedaled so easy and slow down the lanes,
"Deep tawnie cullour" of sunset
each orb some light left from summer
glowing on brown fall ground,
the persimmons are flowing
on streams of more bike-trucks
til they riffle and back up
alongside a car road
and are spread on the gravel by sellers.

The kind with a crease round the middle,
Tamopan, sweet when soft,
ripening down from the top to the base.
Persimmons and farmers
a long busy line on the roadside,
in season, a bargain, a harvest
of years, the peace of
this autumn again, familiar,
when found by surprise at
the tombs of the dead Ming emperors.
Acres of persimmon orchards
surrounding the tumuli
of kings who saw to it they kept on consuming
even when empty and gone.
The persimmons outlive them,
but up on the hills
where the Great Wall wanders
the oaks had been cut for lumber or charcoal
by Genghis Khan's time.
People and persimmon orchards prevail.
I walked the Great Wall today,
and went deep in the dark of a tomb.
And then found a persimmon
ripe to the bottom
one of a group on a rough plaited tray
that might have been drawn by Mu Ch'i,
tapping its infant-soft skin
to be sure that it's ready,
the old man laughing,
he sees that I like my persimmons.
I trade him some coin
for this wealth of fall fruit

lined up on the roadside to sell to the tourists
who have come to see tombs,
and are offered as well
the people and trees that prevail.

Beijing, Peoples Republic

Tiny Energies

VII

1970–1984

For such situations of a few combinations found in messages, the energy content as a fuel is far too negligible to measure or consider compared to the great flows of energy in the food chain. Yet the quality of this energy (tiny energies in the right form) is so high that in the right control circuit it may obtain huge amplifications and control vast flows of power.

H.T. Odum, *Environment Power and Society*

Dragonfly

Dragonfly
Dead on the snow
How did you come so high
Did you leave your seed child
In a mountain pool
Before you died

Evolution Basin IX 69

Through

The white spot of a Flicker
    receding through cedar

Fluttering red surveyors tapes
    through trees, the dark woods

Spring

bees humming

tires spinning

spring mud

For Berkeley

City of buds and flowers

Where are your fruits?

Where are your roots.

The Songs at Custer's Battlefield

Crickets and meadowlarks today;

    that day—

"Some lovers wake one day"

Some lovers wake one day
To a stone wall in the way
—I should be free to choose—
Mutually accuse.
The rest is years to tell:
Domestic hell.

"What history fails to mention is"

What history fails to mention is

Most everybody lived their lives
With friends and children, played it cool,
Left truth & beauty to the guys
Who tricked for bigshots, and were fools.

Channelled Scablands

Asleep on an eight foot strip of grass
In Eastern Washington
A thousand square miles
Of plowed wheatfield.

The Taste

I don't know where it went
Or recall how it worked
What one did
What the steps were
Was it hands?
Or the words and the tune?
All that's left
Is a flavor
That stays

Home on the Range

Bison rumble-belly
Bison shag coat
Bison sniffing bison body
Bison skull looking at the sweat lodge.
Bison liver warm. Bison flea
Bison paunch stew.
Bison baby falls down.
Bison skin home. Bison bedding,
"Home on the Range."

The Forest Fire at Ananda

A skunk walks out of a thicket
      of burning blackberries

And down the hill come hundreds of
      yellow–clad firefighters

After fire, green
sprouts

many children

of the same old roots

The Route

We didn't go so much to the south
As to the west.
Following the hills
Beating the bad
Greeting the good.

The Other Side of Each Coin

The head of a man of the ruling elite
And a very large building.
One on each side of the coin

Serves

A human arm
bone is the best
bone for a
bone chisel.
A corn cob
serves as a cork.

(As stated by: Captain Cook, and an elder lady of Zuni.)

W

in every house there is a wife
in every wife there is a womb
in every womb there is a waif
in every waif there is a wail
in every wail there is a will

The Net

A man in a canoe
Catching fish by dancing—

    "hey, fish by casting with a net!"

Women in the evening circle
casting, round a fire

A man in a canoe
Dances with a net.

Tibetan Army Surplus Store

—The Tibetan Army knife,
With a special patented
Mind-opener,

Used Dorjes,
With the wrong number of prongs.

"Lots of play"

Lots of play

in the way things work,
in the way things are.

History is made of mistakes.

yet—on the surface—
the world looks OK

lots of play.

The Orchard

Writhing, wreathing,
The twang of a fence drawn up tight.

Pound, pound, the staples go in
Gates on hinges—

Sakura to bloom, persimmon leafing out.

Know

The trees know
stars to be sources

Like the sun,
of their life;

But many   and tiny
sprinkled through the dark

When,
where has the sun gone—

Gatha for All Threatened Beings

Ah Power that swirls us together
Grant us bliss
Grant us the great release
And to all beings
Vanishing, wounded,
In trouble on earth,
We pass on this love
May their numbers increase

"There are those who love to get dirty"

There are those who love to get dirty
    and fix things.
They drink coffee at dawn,
    beer after work,

And those who stay clean,
    just appreciate things,
At breakfast they have milk
    and juice at night.

There are those who do both,
    they drink tea.

Lizards, Wind, Sunshine, Apples

a plane circling in the distance
a football game on the radio in the barn
an axe chopping in the woods
a chicken pecking catfood in the kitchen.

How Zen Masters Are Like Mature Herring

So few become full grown
And how necessary all the others;
     gifts to the food chain,
      feeding another universe.

These big ones feed sharks.

Satires, Inventions, & Diversions

VIII

1951–1980

Villanelle of the Wandering Lapps

We seek the hidden lair
Where the strange beast goes—
The honey-footed bear.

With a cruel gold snare
We track him in the snow—
We seek the hidden lair.

The bleak winds blare
Where the bald moon glows
The honey-footed bear,

Was born, soft and fair,
With a wet pink nose.
We seek the hidden lair.

But he ate the bright glare,
So fierce did he grow
The honey-footed bear,

Of the sun in the air.
And the grassland froze.
We seek the hidden lair
Of the honey-footed bear.

The Professor as Transformer

That ugly infant who stole sunshine
from the Old Man's lodge
dances in impotent rage: children,
feed him! lest he loose light,
      blinding us with imponderables.
who could have guessed his love
for putrid fish?

That Greasy Boy with knowledge,
naked, and dull as mush,
   a REAL SEDUCER
The outraged girl protests—
"But Mother, he ———"
"Hush child, he cured you didn't he?"
      (we wash our hair in urine in this town)

"I am enormous,
Wonders cower in my beak
Come, guess what I will say!"
Feed him. he ate the belly of his slave.

caw
caw
the bleak didactic cry

Bloomington
182

The Elusiad
Or Culture Still Uncaught
IN HEROICKS

Fair *Clio*, of the muses most severe,
Calliope, Erato, my song hear:
Of *Culture*, and her various complex ways
That tangle *Man* in folly all his days.

Each soul from dawn to dark each act behaves
In *Culture's* net, unseen; yet he who braves
Some deed beyond her shaping soon will know
Sad guilt, remorse, and social outcast's woe.

Stout *Lowie* "rags and patches" thus described
Of *Culture's* various workings, *Benedict* bribed
By false *Gestalt* and ugly *Structure's* name
Proclaimed a *Pattern* in her all the same;
But brave *Sapir* a manly tear once shed;
Saw *Culture* as man's most Procrustean bed.

Hence *Students*, bending all their thoughts to map
Bleak *Culture's* Protean name will find mayhap
Their subject swift transform from hideous hag
To shining youth, a fire, a leathern bag
And leave them sunk in ign'rance as before—
Perplex'd, bewilder'd, seldom knowing more.
But lo! The hunters have a happy thought,

To trap dim *Culture's* form, say what she's not!
Restrictions six are cunningly designed—
A noose to drop on *Culture* from behind.
Behaviour then becomes the Goddess' name
And her confusing shapes are called the same.

But in the bosky wood a figure lurks—
'Tis *Language* still untrapp'd, who does her works
In *Culture's* guise, applies a mantic frame
To lines & figures, making charms to tame
Rude uncouth sounds to *Meaning* cruel and clear,
So man a moral in all chatt'ring hears.
This mystick force of *Language* sure must prove
It false to put her in *Behaviour's* groove—
Yet *Language* often goes in *Culture's* dress;
The two are but one Goddess, this distress
Allows our captur'd *Culture* to escape
And join the lurking figure; in one shape
A radiant Maiden stands, and students gape.

"Bring more restrictions!" is the hearty cry
And armed with spears of "never, no, & why"
They scatter through the land, proclaim in glee
At ev'ry new glimps'd figure, "That's not she!"
Poor pious madmen, seeking all their days,
When ev'n the search is under *Culture's* gaze.

For she, cruel Goddess! Speaks to our surprise—
"Ev'n seeking me, you see through Mine own eyes."

The Third Watch

He is the pard that pads on two bare feet,
Plucks the sacred seventh of his bow
Twangs air to ashes in a heat.

Then rising tide-wash lips the clean cool rocks:
Who but the Lover floats off-shore in surf?
Her cockle-shell is but a pudding crust,

Her known erotic zone a source of mirth.
Or change the trope: with water, night, and dream
Select the mythical fable of your "soul."

No one will snicker if you toss and scream
At monsters of the amniotic brain—
But if a barefoot stranger in their midst,

Sacred lions, swans, and limping bull
Choose him to charge: who wanders through their den
And turns the rose, or idol, or slow chant

Into a mock of that mock-awful night.
Furious Aphrodite casts her glance
Beyond Eorthan Modor's steamy lair

Where he, the Buddha, walks. Rattle of hooves and horns,
Nets and knives, falls on an empty air
—Something is awake once walked in there.

Sestina of the End of the Kalpa

You joyous Gods, who gave mankind his Culture,
And you, brave nymphs, who taught him love of Nature,
You sturdy Mountains, Prairies, in your Pattern
Breeding from Uncouth Ape the various Races,
Give ear to what I sing, of place and Structure,
Troubling the simple air with blushing Language.

Because, astride his horse, a Siouan's Language
As well as painted steed, is part of Culture,
We soon find Substance melted into Structure.
And pitying poor Mankind's silly Nature—
An equal meagre blandness in all Races:
We look beyond mere Man to find a Pattern.

Each blotch and wiggle has distinctive Pattern,
And order lurks within each mumbling Language.
Hermes the sneaky watcher of the Races,
If caught might tell the sins of every Culture.
Each bungles life according to its Nature,
Which is to say, each has a faulty Structure.

But Man is taught necessity of Structure,
And Birth and Death whirl in a single Pattern;
The bleating Dewey says, "But this is Nature"—
And Law and Order, if you know the Language.
To have a God (The Possum sez) is Culture,
And God is Order, for most Human Races.

Apollo: let us wander through the Races,
Sifting each hiss and glottal for its Structure,
And come to make conclusion of all Culture.
Poor Kwakiutl! Tangled in their Pattern;
Stern Indo-Aryans; slaves to Language.
And somehow through this, Science fingers Nature.

A use is found for every law of Nature,
The future planned (humanely) for all Races,
Wisdom wallows in decay of Language.
Fierce *Siva*! These Greeks defend their "Structure,"
The God of Christians, in the same old Pattern
Perpetuates the form and force of Culture,

Destroyer: with fire inform the Races
That Chaos is the Pattern under Structure.
Language and Culture burn! and death to Nature.

Berkeley

Epistemological Fancies

My friend Hoodlatch used to ask,
"Can these five senses know the real?"
Perceive the Ground, or God, or What
Is felt when these five senses feel?"

And two would do, I used to say,
To crack through what illusions might
Out-side our senses to wrong scent
Or baffle heard or heart insight—

"And just what two?" He'd often jeer:
Profundity and clear precept
Obstructed by (we thought) the sense
That wades in superficial depth—

Why any two, or all, or none,
Will do to put the Noumenon
In its right place: which is in front
Of wispy, frail phenomenon.

For all that's real, or ought to be,
Is what one can, or cannot, see.

A War of Dwarfs and Birds Beyond the Sea

Feeble breakers, the loose kelp slop
Slopping in swarm of squid, a warm beach.
Care, carry it in your head without words,
We have ways, waves of talking about the sea.

Apprehensive, in to the waist,
The shy ones urinate in the sea.

What we file, defile, is tern-pipe
Seasnipe, drowned mews, bird fright:
A grammar of scattered cries.
One tells a file, a system, to the sea.

This utterance is oblivious of the sea
Wet, of course, but water? in the sea?

It takes a net, a swatch of labels wagging
With the jawbone, the *Sea* is made tongue
Tickling a rush of air behind the teeth,
A high front moan; and now you understand.

Exclamations Gone to the
Twin Breasts of Maya

Terence! Ovid! Nothing is satisfactory.
Bleeding the fluvial ground to raise grape, pay tax—
Vag rap sufferings, the hard bust rock,
And all who knew you gone on the last witch-
Angel Diesel-hike, the metaphysical
Home gate she made wild.

Ballad of Rolling Heads

Here's the last drunk song I'll sing
Of all the balls we had this Spring.
Swigging Akadama Port,
Holding my Kyoto fort
Against the waves of squares and scholars
That truss me up in ties and collars;
Shavehead Roshis put to bed
Like babies simple in the head;
An arty nation plunged in squalor
That never learned to jump or holler—
In my wine I'll gently float
Back to where I caught the boat
Leaving T and addled brains
In that last campfire in the rain—
Clear back to ancient lost November
High and swinging nights remember:
Jack Kerouac in smoky flame
Blazing bright at Buddha's name,
Sputtering in his jug of port
Cursing Cowley's last report,
Burning hot & bright again
With poems and notes beneath his pen
While Whalen talked precise and clear
Drunk and barefoot on the floor;
Naked Allen, naked Peter,
Neuri in her shoes and sweater,

Montgomery peering through the screen,
Jinnie lovely as a Queen,
The toothless grin of Du Peru
Who saw the whole of wisdom through
And ended wholly baffled simple
Concerned with shoes and socks & pimples,
La Vigne who painted in his head
The orgies held on floors and beds
And who of all of us shall be
The one who saves poor Natalie—
Who finished off this round of pain,
I tracked her through the Bardo plane
Peyote-sick but seeing clear
The hells & heavens we are near.
Neal with pockets full of T
Dirty pictures on his knee
Spread out to view by candlelight—
McCorkle's shack, an April night,
Locke getting off the kids to bed
With sips of Casanova red—
The wine, the wine, the wine is gone!
And Kerouac has left for town
To buy another gallon jug
We'll all be rolled out on the rug—

The wilderness is in the heart
Where babies books & orgies start
With jugs & blankets, dressed in rags
The whole wild tribe is on the vag
From book to book & town to town
& cops or books can't put us down
Until beyond all cures & beds
On floors, on floors we bang our heads

& sing with angels drunk as we
Hung up in the Christmas tree
Of Golden Boughs and Buddha-eyes,
Fertility to make us wise!
This thunderbolt is hard as jewel,
A swinging dink both hot and cool
The opposites are all congealed
& squares and fools will be revealed
By Whalen's calm and classic glance,
Allen Ginsberg's naked dance.

After T'ao Ch'ien

"Swiftly the years, beyond recall:
  Solemn the stillness of this Spring morning."
I'll put on my boots & old levis
& hike across Tamalpais.
Along the coast the fog hovers,
Hovers an hour, then scatters.
There comes a wind, blowing from the sea,
That brushes the hills of spring grass.

marin-an

After the Chinese

She looked like a fairy
All dressed in shaky cheesecloth,
And ran off with a fairy poet
Back to town. Her hair
Was black as a mud-snail's bowels
Her skin was like chilled grease.
My sleeves are sopping wet
From crying. My white hair scraggly
& my eyes all red. Pour another
Cup of wine for this poor
Bureaucrat stuck out in the sticks.

Versions of Anacreon

On his Own Loves
If you can tell the leaves on all the trees
And know all the sands of the sea,
You alone can calculate my loves.
First, for Athens put down twenty and add fifteen;
Great lists of loves for Corinth, which is Achaia,
Where women are fair.
Then put my Lesbian, and the far Ionians,
And Caria and Rhodes—two thousand loves.
                    You say What? Add more:
I haven't mentioned my Syrian, my passions at Canopus,
Or those of Crete—where everything happens—
Love holds orgies in the streets.
                    What?
You want the count of those beyond Gadira,
And the Bactrians, and the Indians,
Loves of my soul?

To a Girl
Don't run off because my hair is gray
Don't put me down because your
            first fresh flower-young beauty's with you.
Look: even in garlands
It is good to see the white lilies
Twined with roses.

On Himself

　　　WHEN I drink wine,
My warmed heart hears the Muses.
　　　When I drink wine,
Cares fall away, and busy thinking
And contriving becomes wind beating the sea.
　　　When I drink wine,
Sorrow-melting Bacchus whirls me
In flowery breezes, charmed and delirious.
　　　When I drink wine,
I weave rings of flowers and
Put them on my head, and sing the calm-of-life.
　　　When I drink wine,
My body sprinkled in perfume,
Clasping a girl in my arms, I sing of Venus.
　　　When I drink wine,
Out of embossed cups, soothing my soul,
I delight in a choir of youths.
　　　When I drink wine,
This is the only gain. I've taken it,
And I'll carry it away.
For after all, we have to die.

On Love

It hurts to love
It hurts not to love
It hurts worst to fail at love.
Birth is nothing to love:
Wisdom, genius, get tramped down.
They look to money alone.
Money breaks up brothers,
Money breaks up parents,

Causes wars and murders.
What is worse,
Money kills us lovers.

A Little Ode on Lovers
Horses have the print of fire
                   on their haunches:
Anyone can tell a Parthian by his turban.
And I can tell lovers on sight:
They have a certain delicate
Impress of the soul
Within.

(From John Taylor's literal interlinear.)

Tree Song

Between dirt dark and giddy sky
Straight, twisted, mountains, mudflats,
Where we bloom,
     limbs that wait and wave,
Noble Silence for a lifetime's talk.

     across the hill the pollen blows
     a cloud of orgies in the boughy air—

Are we our black wet roots
Or do we live by light?
One hand grips, the other makes a sign.
Scanning slope or gully where it soon must lie.

     I lay
This punky mossy gnarled and
Useless scab-barked worm-ate
Seedless wore out loggy body
—with a great crash—
              down.
My secret heartwood no bud ever knew.

   Kyoto

Joe Hill Fragment

"The copper bosses shot you Joe—"

    sheets of color shift like northern lights.
    the tiger grumbles in the bamboo grove
    streetcars squeak to carbarns in the night.
    sending signals, scaring fish,
    tankers wallow in the sea
    the Hungry Ghosts and Demons out on strike—

"I never died" said he.

Prepotent

Justin Morgan
    was powerful and large.
J.M. didn't look a
    bit like his Maw or Paw.
He was born Springfield Mass
    about 1790,
He once won a gallon of rum
    on a bet.
He made love
    all over New England.
All his children grew up
    strong and strange as he.
We still see them sometimes,
    those Morgans.

Hieiharu-maru

A Work for Burke

"Moveable type" indeed has spread the Word
& printers' devils mightier than swords.
In China first, the Diamond Sutra pressed
With type of clay, all Sentient Beings Blessed.

Gunpowder & compass, to Europe gift
Along with printing, brought about a shift
From Feudal to Bourgeois. From Asia
On Mongol ponies' backs. The phase you

See us enter now, post-industry
Replete with glamorous technology
Will nonetheless need PRINTING all the more
For keeping track, and evening the score.

Printing, with beauty, craft and skill,
In any age brings deep aesthetic thrills
To watchful minds. We must not shirk
Support of Cranium Press, & Clifford Burke.

(written at the eminent Printer's request)

smog

smog

smog

smog

smog   smog   smog

smog   smog   smog

smog   smog   smog   smog   smog

smog   smog   smog   smog   smog

smog smog smog smog smog smog smog smog

smog smog smog smog smog smog smog smog smog

smog smog smog smog smog smog smog smog smog

Sherry in July

Julius Caesar, cut from his mother's womb
    Caedare to cut off (caesura)
    Sanskrit *khidāti*—tear—
(Jack Wilson, Wovoka, Paiute "Cutter")
Caesar to Kaiser to Tsesari, Tsar.
    and a town in Spain, Caesaris
    —Xeres—Jerez—
    have some sherry.

Coyote Man, Mr. President, & the Gunfighters

Mr. President was fascinated by gunfighters. Expert gunfighters were invited to his White House, three thousand of them, like guests in the house. Day and night they practiced fast-draw and shootouts in his presence until the dead and wounded men numbered more than a hundred a year.

The Senator from the Great Basin was troubled by this, and summoning his aides, said, "I'll give a basket of turquoise and a truckload of compost to any man who can reason with Mr. President and make him give up these gunfights!" "Coyote Man is the one who can do it!" said his aides.

Pretty soon Coyote Man turned up, but he refused the turquoise. He said, "If Mr. President should get angry, I might go to jail. What could I do with turquoise then? And if I do persuade him, then you'd owe a million wild ducks."

"The trouble is," said the Senator, "Mr. President refuses to see anybody but gunfighters." "Fine!" said Coyote Man, "I'm good with revolvers."

"But the kind of gunfighters Mr. President receives," said the Senator, "all wear starched uniforms and have shaved cheeks; they glare fiercely, and speak in staccato sentences about ballistics and tactical deployment. Men like that he loves! If you go in to see him in your overalls you'd be wrong from the start."

"I'll get me the uniform of a gunfighter," said Coyote Man. After a couple of days he had his gunfighter's costume ready and arranged an appointment with Mr. President. Mr. President's guards had their big Magnum revolvers on Coyote Man as he entered calm and soft. "Now that you got the Senator to get you an appointment what do you think you can tell me?" said Mr. President.

"I heard Mr. President likes guns, and so I have come to demonstrate my skill to you."
"What's special about your skill?" said Mr. President. "My shooting strikes and kills at every shot, and doesn't miss at nine hundred miles," said Coyote Man.

Mr. President was pleased and said, "I'd like to see you shoot it out." Coyote Man said, "He who draws the revolver plucks out emptiness, teases on with hopes of dominance. Leaves last, arrives first. Allow me to show my capacity."

Mr. President spent a week checking out his gunfighters. Three dozen were wounded or died in the trials. The survivors were instructed to appear on the lawn and Mr. President sent for Coyote Man.

"Today let's see you reach for the revolver with these fine officers. What will you shoot? A long or a short barrel?"

"I'll use any type," said Coyote Man. "It happens I have three revolvers. You tell me which to use—but first I'll explain them."

"Let's hear about your three revolvers," said Mr. President.

"There is the revolver of the cosmos, the revolver of mankind, and the revolver of state."

"What is the revolver of the cosmos?" asked Mr. President. —"The revolver of the cosmos? The Milky Way is its grip; the solar winds, the barrel. Its bullets are stars, it sights by the beams of pulsars. It spits out planets and bathes them, spinning, in heat and light. The ninety-two elements aim it; the secrets of fusion fire it. Wield it, and countless beings leap into life and dance through the void. Conceal it, and whole galaxies rush into nothingness. When this revolver is manifested the whole earth flourishes, the skies clear, the rivers sing, the gardens are full of squash and corn, the high plains rich with Bison. This is the revolver of the cosmos."

Mr. President was at an utter loss. "So what is the revolver of mankind?"

"The revolver of mankind? The twelve races are the grip; the three thousand languages, the barrel. Forged in the Pliocene, finished in the Pleistocene, decorated with civilization, it aims for knowledge and beauty. The cylinder is the rise and fall of nations, the sights are the philosophies and religions and sciences, the bullets are countless men and women who have pierced through ignorance and old habits, and revealed the shining mirror of true nature. It takes its model from life itself, and trusts in the four seasons. Its secret power is the delight of the mind. Once grasped it brings harmony and peace to the planet; like a thunderbolt it destroys exploiters, and dictators crumble like sand. This is the revolver of mankind."

Mr. President said, "What is the revolver of the State?"

"The revolver of the State? It is used by men in starched uniforms with shaved chins who glare fiercely and speak in staccato sentences about ballistics and tactical deployment. On top it blows out brains and splinters neckbones; underneath it spits out livers and lungs. Those who use this revolver are no different from fighting cocks—any morning they may be dead or in jail. They are of no use in the councils of mankind. Now you occupy the office of Mr. President, and yet you show this fondness for gunfighters. I think it is rather unworthy of you."

Mr. President took Coyote Man to the dining room and the waiter brought lunch. But Mr. President just paced around the room. "Hey!" said Coyote Man, "Eat your lunch! The affair of the gunfighters is over and finished!"

After that Mr. President didn't come out of the Oval Room for three months. All his gunfighters secretly took off their uniforms and sneaked away, back to the businesses and offices in various towns around the land from which they had come.

special thanks to Burton Watson.

(After the "Discourse on Swords" in the Third Century BC Chinese Chuang-tzu *text.)*

Design by David Bullen
Typeset in Mergenthaler Bembo
by Harrington-Young
Printed by Maple-Vail
on acid-free paper